Your Favorite Color Has a Meaning

by

Tracy Edwards-Wright

Lulu

Lulu Enterprises, Inc.

Raleigh, North Carolina

Your Favorite Color Has a Meaning

First Printing

Printed in the United States of America

Published by Lulu Enterprises

3101 Hillsborough Street

Raleigh, NC 27607

www.lulu.com

Softcover

ISBN 978-1-105-32366-9

CONTENTS

PREFACE

The usage of colors has a profound effect on communication. Various colors affect moods, feelings, and emotions. It is a phenomenal communication tool and can be used to influence mood and cause psychological reactions such as the color purple which is romantic. Purple also denotes luxury, royalty, and sophistication. Additionally, gold symbolizes wealth, good health, and success. Whether we're a wealthy gold, or a tranquil blue, our color preferences are a key to comprehending our personalities. You are invited to find out what the author has to say about your favorite color, how it affects your feelings, and also, how it brings clarity to who you really are.

~~~*Red*~~~

Red is the color of fire and blood, so it is associated with energy, war, danger, strength, power, determination as well as passion, desire, and love.

Red is a very emotionally intense color. It enhances human metabolism, increases respiration rate, and raises blood pressure. It has very high visibility, which is why stop signs, stoplights, and fire equipment are usually painted red. In heraldry, red is used to indicate courage. It is a color found in many national flags.

Red brings text and images to the foreground. Use it as an accent color to stimulate people to make quick decisions; it is a perfect color for 'Buy Now' or 'Click Here' buttons on Internet banners and websites. In advertising, red is often used to evoke erotic feelings (red lips, red nails, red-light districts, 'Lady in Red', etc). Red is widely used to indicate danger (high voltage signs, traffic lights). This color is also commonly associated with energy, so you can use it when promoting energy drinks, games, cars, and items related to sports and high physical activity.

Light red represents joy, sexuality, passion, sensitivity, and love.

Dark red is associated with vigor, willpower, rage, anger, leadership, courage, longing, malice, and wrath.

Reddish-brown is associated with harvest and fall.

~~~*Orange*~~~

Orange combines the energy of red and the happiness of yellow. It is associated with joy, sunshine, and the tropics. Orange represents enthusiasm, fascination, happiness, creativity, determination, attraction, success, encouragement, and stimulation.

To the human eye, orange is a very hot color, so it gives the sensation of heat. Nevertheless, orange is not as aggressive as red. Orange increases oxygen supply to the brain, produces an invigorating effect, and stimulates mental activity. It is highly accepted among young people. As a citrus color, orange is associated with healthy food and stimulates appetite. Orange is the color of fall and harvest. In heraldry, orange is symbolic of strength and endurance.

Orange has very high visibility, so you can use it to catch attention and highlight the most important elements of your design. Orange is very effective for promoting food products and toys.

Dark orange can mean deceit and distrust.

Red-orange corresponds to desire, sexual passion, pleasure, domination, aggression, and thirst for action.

Gold evokes the feeling of prestige. The meaning of gold is illumination, wisdom, and wealth. Gold often symbolizes high quality.

~~~*Yellow*~~~

Yellow is the color of sunshine. It's associated with joy, happiness, intellect, and energy.

Yellow produces a warming effect, arouses cheerfulness, stimulates mental activity, and generates muscle energy. Yellow is often associated with food. Bright, pure yellow is an attention getter, which is the reason taxicabs are painted this color. When overused, yellow may have a disturbing effect; it is known that babies cry more in yellow rooms. Yellow is seen before other colors when placed against black; this combination is often used to issue a warning. In heraldry, yellow indicates honor and loyalty. Later the meaning of yellow was connected with cowardice.

Use yellow to evoke pleasant, cheerful feelings. You can choose yellow to promote children's products and items related to leisure. Yellow is very effective for attracting attention, so use it to highlight the most important elements of your design. Men usually perceive yellow as a very lighthearted, 'childish' color, so it is not recommended to use yellow when selling prestigious, expensive products to men – nobody will buy a yellow business suit or a yellow Mercedes. Yellow is an unstable and spontaneous color, so avoid using yellow if you want to suggest stability and safety. Light yellow tends to disappear into white, so it usually needs a dark color to highlight it. Shades of yellow are visually unappealing because they lose cheerfulness and become dingy.

Dull (dingy) yellow represents caution, decay, sickness, and jealousy.

Light yellow is associated with intellect, freshness, and joy.

~~~*Green*~~~

Green is the color of nature. It symbolizes growth, harmony, freshness, and fertility. Green has strong emotional correspondence with safety. Dark green is also commonly associated with money.

Green has great healing power. It is the most restful color for the human eye; it can improve vision. Green suggests stability and endurance. Sometimes green denotes lack of experience; for example, a 'greenhorn' is a novice. In heraldry, green indicates growth and hope. Green, as opposed to red, means safety; it is the color of free passage in road traffic.

Use green to indicate safety when advertising drugs and medical products. Green is directly related to nature, so you can use it to promote 'green' products. Dull, darker green is commonly associated with money, the financial world, banking, and Wall Street.

Dark green is associated with ambition, greed, and jealousy.

Yellow-green can indicate sickness, cowardice, discord, and jealousy.

Aqua is associated with emotional healing and protection.

Olive green is the traditional color of peace.

~~~*Blue*~~~

Blue is the color of the sky and sea. It is often associated with depth and stability. It symbolizes trust, loyalty, wisdom, confidence, intelligence, faith, truth, and heaven.

Blue is considered beneficial to the mind and body. It slows human metabolism and produces a calming effect. Blue is strongly associated with tranquility and calmness. In heraldry, blue is used to symbolize piety and sincerity.

You can use blue to promote products and services related to cleanliness (water purification filters, cleaning liquids, and vodka), air and sky (airlines, airports, and air conditioners), water and sea (sea voyages, mineral water). As opposed to emotionally warm colors like red, orange, and yellow; blue is linked to consciousness and intellect. Use blue to suggest precision when promoting high-tech products.

Blue is a masculine color; according to studies, it is highly accepted among males. Dark blue is associated with depth, expertise, and stability; it is a preferred color for corporate America.

Avoid using blue when promoting food and cooking, because blue suppresses appetite. When used together with warm colors like yellow or red, blue can create high-impact, vibrant designs; for example, blue-yellow-red is a perfect color scheme for a superhero.

Light blue is associated with health, healing, tranquility, understanding, and softness.

Dark blue represents knowledge, power, integrity, and seriousness.

~~~*Purple*~~~

Purple combines the stability of blue and the energy of red. Purple is associated with royalty. It symbolizes power, nobility, luxury, and ambition. It conveys wealth and extravagance. Purple is associated with wisdom, dignity, independence, creativity, mystery, and magic.

According to surveys, almost 75 percent of pre-adolescent children prefer purple to all other colors. Purple is a very rare color in nature; some people consider it to be artificial.

Light purple is a good choice for a feminine design. You can use bright purple when promoting children's products.

Light purple evokes romantic and nostalgic feelings.

Dark purple evokes gloom and sad feelings. It can cause frustration.

~~~*White*~~~

White is associated with light, goodness, innocence, purity, and virginity. It is considered to be the color of perfection.

White means safety, purity, and cleanliness. As opposed to black, white usually has a positive connotation. White can represent a successful beginning. In heraldry, white depicts faith and purity.

In advertising, white is associated with coolness and cleanliness because it's the color of snow. You can use white to suggest simplicity in high-tech products. White is an appropriate color for charitable organizations; angels are usually imagined wearing white clothes. White is associated with hospitals, doctors, and sterility, so you can use white to suggest safety when promoting medical products. White is often associated with low weight, low-fat food, and dairy products.

~~~*Black*~~~

The color black is associated with power, elegance, formality, death, evil, and mystery.

Black is a mysterious color associated with fear and the unknown (black holes). It usually has a negative connotation (blacklist, black humor, 'black death'). Black denotes strength and authority; it is considered to be a very formal, elegant, and prestigious color (black tie, black Mercedes). In heraldry, black is the symbol of grief.

Black gives the feeling of perspective and depth, but a black background diminishes readability. A black suit or dress can make you look thinner. When designing for a gallery of art or photography, you can use a black or gray background to make the other colors stand out. Black contrasts well with bright colors. Combined with red or orange – other very powerful colors – black gives a very aggressive color scheme.

~~*Brown*~~~

Brown symbolizes earth, stability, hearth, home, outdoors, reliability, comfort, endurance, simplicity, and comfort. People who prefer brown are often conventional and orderly. The negative meaning of brown can be a repressed personality or a lazy person. Brown is the color of the earth and is associated with the material side of life. **Brown** also suggests stability and denotes masculine qualities.

Brown Energy

Brown can mix into many surroundings. It is a mixture of red, blue and yellow and has many shades and tones - each producing a different effect. Brown can be a stabilizing color. The red in brown gives it practical energy while the yellow and blue add mental focus energies. Too much brown can make a dull effect. Brown gives a feeling of solidity, and allows one to stay in the background, unnoticed.

Some shades of brown create a warm, comfortable feeling of wholesomeness, naturalness and dependability.

Put some brown in your life when you want:

- **a solid wholesome feeling**

- **to blend with the background**

- **a connection with natural earth and the stability this brings**

- **orderliness and convention**

Brown gem stone properties

Brown gemstones act as a grounding force and promote stability and clear thinking.

~~~*Silver*~~~

Silver symbolizes security, reliability, intelligence, staid, modesty, dignity, maturity, solid, conservative, practical, old age, sadness, boring. Silver symbolizes calm. Silver is a mineral that is said to mirror the soul, strengthen the connection between astral and physical bodies, and enhance intuitive and psychic energies.

Silver is mystically considered to improve speech, bring eloquence. It is also purported to attract, enhance and store the energies of gemstones, as well as draw out negative energies.

Silver is related to the moon, and moon energies.

Silver, especially shiny, metallic silver, is cool like gray but livelier, more playful. Silver can be sleek and modern or impart a feeling of ornate riches. Silver is a precious metal and other metals are often described as silver in color. Silver doesn't have the warmth of gold. It's a cool metal. Silver often symbolizes riches, just as gold does. Silver can be glamorous and distinguished. While gray-haired men and women are seen as old, silver-haired denotes a graceful aging. Silver is the traditional Twenty-Fifth Wedding Anniversary gift.

Keywords for Meaning of Silver:

glamorous, distinguishment, high tech, industrial, graceful aging, telepathy, clairvoyance, clairaudience, psychometry, intuition, dreams, astral energies, female power, communication, goddess, ornate riches, sleekness, modernity.

~~~*Pink*~~~

Pink is the color of universal love. Pink is a quiet color. Lovers of beauty favor pink. A pink carnation means "I will never forget you".

Pink Energy

Pink is a combination of red and white. The quality of energy in pink is determined by how much red is present. White is the potential for fullness, while red helps you to achieve that potential. Pink combines these energies. Shades of deep pink, such as magenta, are effective in neutralizing disorder and violence. Some prisons use limited deep pink tones to diffuse aggressive behavior. Pink also signifies romance, love, and friendship. It denotes feminine qualities and passiveness.

Pink provides feelings of caring, tenderness, self-worth and love, acceptance.

Put some pink in your life when you want:

- **calm feelings**

- **to neutralize disorder**

- **relaxation**

- **acceptance, contentment**

21

Pink gem stone properties

Pink gemstones can be used to promote love, self-worth, order and protection from violence or aggression. Carry or place pink gemstones around your home or office to stimulate love and beauty.

Wearing Pink

Wear pink when you want to present yourself as a peaceful, calm person who is not threatening. The softer shades are very feminine and darker shades will alleviate feelings of friction.

~~~*Gray*~~~

Gray is the color of sorrow. People who favor gray can be the lone wolf type or narrow-minded. Gray with more silver in it can be a very active color.

Native Americans associate gray with friendship. Gray is the symbol for security, maturity and dependability. It connotes responsibility and conservative practicality.

Gray Energy

Gray is the true neutral color. Its energy imparts void, emptiness, lack of movement, emotion, warmth and identifying characteristics. Because of this, gray can be restful. It has a detached and isolated feeling. Gray can have a cooling effect when placed next to other more vibrant colors. It has a stabilizing effect, making vibrant colors stand out while muting their vibration.

Put some gray in your life when you want:

- **to emphasize your willingness to comply**
- **a neutral, non-invasive feeling**
- **to reduce the intense energy of another color**
- **to feel detached or isolated**

Gray gem stone properties

Gray gemstones are healing stones and can assist in improving relationships toward more stability.

Wearing Gray

Gray clothing suggests efficiency and is often used for this in the business world. Gray can also suggest lack of imagination, so should be used carefully. Gray will emphasize neutrality. Too much gray, or the wrong shades will suggest lack of character, initiative and detachment. Add a hint of another color to gray clothing to express efficiency with personality.

~~~*Gold*~~~

It is no surprise that gold symbolizes wealth used wisely, but it is also the symbol of good health. People who favor the color gold are optimistic.

Gold Energy

The Tibetan Buddhist believes in 5 sacred stones: the crystal for light, turquoise for infinity of sea and sky, coral for life and form, gold for the golden ray of the sun, silver for the light of the moon. Gold is intimately linked with Divinity and those gods associated with the Sun. It symbolizes wealth and success.

Put some gold in your life when you want:

- increased personal power

- relaxation and enjoyment of life

- good health

- success

Wearing Gold

Wearing gold in everyday life increases personal power, and promotes courage, confidence and willpower. Gold chains worn around the neck preserve health.

~~~*Burgundy*~~~

When using the color Burgundy, energy healing brings fierce power, confrontations, and explosive energies.

The Energy Healing Properties of the Color Burgundy give you great strength of character. It means that you need to stand up for yourself, a cause or another.

The meanings of Burgundy Energy tell us that it is time to make a plan and make a stand, call in your allies, know if you have any. Use the Energy Healing Properties of the Color Burgundy when you need to pull up your deepest power reserves, your thigh strength, dig in your heels and confront that bully, for you are empowered for victory.

Key Words for Energy Healing with the Color Burgundy:

- Power Reserves

- Attack or be Attacked

- Battle- Confront Bullies

- Thigh Chakra

- Deep Strength

- Allies, Strategy

~~~*Turquoise*~~~

Turquoise helps to open the lines of communication between the heart and the spoken word. It presents as a friendly and happy color enjoying life.

In color psychology, the color turquoise controls and heals the emotions creating emotional balance and stability. In the process it can appear to be on an emotional roller coaster, up and down, until it balances itself.

A combination of blue and a small amount of yellow, turquoise fits in on the color scale between green and blue. It radiates the peace, calm and tranquility of blue and the balance and growth of green with the uplifting energy of yellow.

Turquoise recharges our spirits during times of mental stress and tiredness, alleviating feelings of loneliness. You only have to focus on the color turquoise, whether on a wall or clothing and you feel instant calm and gentle invigoration, ready to face the world again!

Turquoise is a great color to have around you, particularly in an emergency, as it helps with clear thinking and decision-making. It assists in the development of organizational and management skills. It influences rather than preaching and demanding.

The color turquoise is a good color to aid concentration and clarity of thought for public speakers as it calms the nervous system, gives control over speech and expression, and builds confidence. Print your speech notes on turquoise and every time you glance down you will feel the effects of the color.

Turquoise heightens levels of creativity and sensitivity. It is good at multi-tasking, becoming bored if forced to focus on one thing only. Sometimes its thinking can become scattered if surrounded by too much of this balancing color.

Turquoise encourages inner healing through its ability to enhance empathy and caring. It heightens our intuitive ability and opens the door to spiritual growth. It is the color of the evolved soul.

Turquoise can also be self-centered, tuning in to its own needs above all others. At the same time, it can help us to build our self-esteem and to love ourselves, which in turn supports our ability to love others unconditionally. At its most extreme it can be boastful and narcissistic. Turquoise is a good color to use when you are stuck in a rut and don't know which way to move.

Too much turquoise in your life may give you an overactive mind and create emotional imbalance, making you either over-emotional or non-emotional.

Too little turquoise in your life may cause you to withhold your emotions, resulting in secrecy and confusion about your direction in life.

From a negative perspective, the meaning of the color turquoise relates to being either over-emotional or non-emotional, lacking communication skills, being unreliable and deceptive.

Positive and Negative Traits of Turquoise

Positive keywords include communication, clarity of thought, balance and harmony, idealism, calmness, creativity, compassion, healing and self-sufficiency.

Negative keywords include boastfulness, secrecy, unreliability and reticence, fence-sitting, aloofness, deception and off-handedness.

The Color Turquoise Represents

Communication: Turquoise represents open communication from and between the heart and the spoken word. It relates to the electronic age and the world of computers, and communication on a large scale.

Emotional Control: Being the mid color between the extremes of red and violet, turquoise is the color of balance, for the emotions, thoughts and speech.

Effects of the Color Turquoise

Clarity of Thought: Turquoise enhances the ability to focus and concentrate, assisting with clear thinking and decision-making, and the development of good organizational skills.

Calming: Turquoise is calming yet invigorating, restoring depleted energies.

Non-emotional: A negative effect of turquoise is that it can cause people to be too aloof and to hide their emotional reactions.

~~~*Indigo*~~~

Indigo is the color of the deep midnight sky. It can have a negative effect when used during a depressed state, because it will deepen the mood. Indigo symbolizes a mystical borderland of wisdom, self-mastery and spiritual realization. While blue is the color of communication with others, indigo turns the blue inward, to increase personal thought, profound insights, and instant understandings. While blue can be fast, indigo is almost instantaneous. Inventors use indigo skills for inspirations that seem to 'come out of the blue'.

Put some indigo in your life when you want:

- **to focus on personal issues**

- **to develop intuition**

- **to step outside of everyday life for a new and interesting way of viewing a problem**

- **solitude and inner communication**

Indigo gem stone properties

Indigo gemstones open the door to the subconscious, symbolizing the bridge between the finite and infinite. They are used as a guide to cosmic knowledge. The indigo stones are indigo, sapphire, and azurite.

References

http://www.color-wheel-pro.com/color-meaning.html

http://crystal-cure.com/color-meanings.html

http://www.princetonol.com/groups/iad/lessons/middle/color2.htm

http://www.old-earth.com/chapter-burgundy.html

http://www.empower-yourself-with-color-psychology.com/color-turquoise.html

http://www.beading-design-jewelry.com/meaning-of-silver.html

http://desktoppub.about.com/cs/colorselection/p/blue.htm

http://www.dreammoods.com/dreamthemes/colors.htm

Other Books Written by the Author

"From Humiliation to Celebration"

"Living to Give: The Gift of Giving"

Visit barnesandnoble.com or amazon.com for more information. Also, for additional ordering options, you may Google the author's name as Tracy Edwards-Wright.

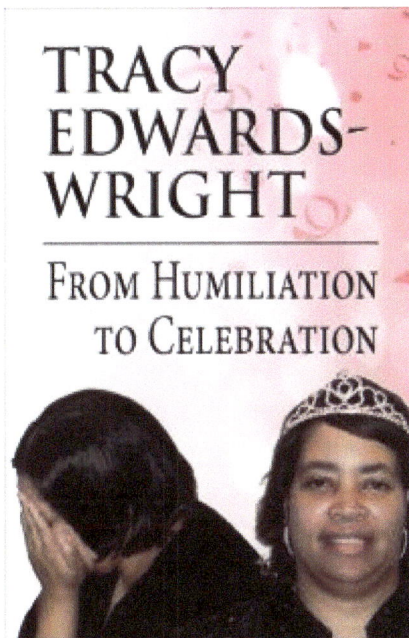

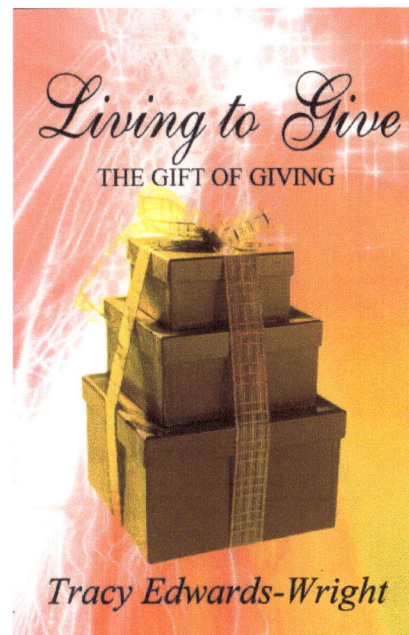